A
Daughter
is a
Gift

To: Wendily

From: Mom

A Daughter is a Gift

Illustrated by Alexis Siroc

WARNER BOOKS

An AOL Time Warner Company

Copyright © 2003 by Redbridge LLC

Illustrations copyright © 2003 by Spinning Plates Studio

Warner Book, Inc., 1271 Avenue of the Americas, New York, NY 10020

Visit our Web site at www.twbookmark.com.

 An AOL Time Warner Company

Printed in the United States of America

First Printing: April 2003

10 9 8 7 6 5 4 3 2 1

Library of Congress Cataloging-in-Publication Data

A daughter is a gift.

    p. cm.

  ISBN 0-446-53118-9

   1. Daughters. 2. Gift books. I. Warner Books (Firm)

  HQ777 .D35 2003

  306.874--dc21

                                             2002033177

Design by Alexis Siroc

If God made anything
better than a girl, He sure
kept it to Himself.

—NELSON ALGREN,
FROM *A WALK ON THE WILD SIDE*

A Daughter is a Gift ✳ 8

The Gift of a Mother's Helper ✳ 16

The Gift of Seeing in the Dark ✳ 23

The Gift of Choosing to Climb ✳ 31

The Gift of a Brave Heart ✳ 38

The Gift of the Dutiful One ✳ 45

The Gift of Endless Possibilities ✳ 50

My Daughter, My Gift: What I Love
Most about My Daughter ✳ 56

A Daughter
is a Gift

*"The finest inheritance you
can give to a child is to allow it to
make its way on its own."*

—ISADORA DUNCAN

*I*magine, if you can, a tiny girl dressed in a pair of pink cotton pajamas who is getting ready to go to bed.

Maybe she's a "mommy" girl who bathes her baby dolls in a little plastic tub before tucking each one into its cradle at night. Or maybe she's a bookish child with a taste for fairy tales about enchanted ponies and magical princesses who live in faraway kingdoms. Perhaps our girl is a temperamental tantrum-thrower who *won't* brush her teeth, *won't* take a bath, and *insists* on staying up late. Though her parents try to quell the rebellion, their steely resolve melts like ice cream when they see her impish face turn fiery red, just as it did the first time they held her in their arms and fell in love. Because, you see, she isn't *any* little girl, she is *their* little girl—their *daughter*. And the moment is perfect.

A daughter is a gift. Whether or not those words have ever drifted through your mind in a quiet moment of deep reflection, the truth is undeniable. A daughter is a gift of extraordinary value. Signifying the hopes and dreams of the parents who gave her life, a daughter is a victory garden where relationships blossom, emotions flourish, and innovative ideas take root. "A Frenchman once wrote that 'daughters are flowers o' the home,'" the father of a newborn recently recalled. "Now that I have a little girl of my own, I understand why."

"daughters are flowers o' the home"

What is it about daughter-hood that creates such mystique, igniting our love and affection? Perhaps the sheer variety of daughters is part of the allure. While one little girl is notoriously a "tomboy" with a passion for climbing trees in her overalls, another is a "mother's little helper" who dons her apron as soon as the first mixing bowl comes out of the cupboard. A "daddy's girl" in shiny black Mary Janes who trails her father around like a lovesick puppy is not to be confused with a bookworm who loves to be alone in the library stacks.

"Modern daughters are amazingly varied," a middle-school teacher said recently. "While some girls are homespun and traditional, others are full of fire and vinegar, blazing new trails with innovation. When you start to generalize about girls, make sure to leave plenty of room for the rugged individuals."

Our teacher is right. For as many daughters as there are who bake cookies, knit sweaters, and run a baby-sitting club, there are just as many who shoot hoops, shoot skeet, and shoot movies. In today's world, womanhood is about reaching one's potential, often in areas long reserved for men. "To be all that you can be," as the saying goes, is a modern daughter's prerogative.

"When our little girl was born," one new dad noted, "I held her in my arms, wondering how her life would unfold. Would she be a rocket scientist—or a culinary artist? A jet pilot—or a nurse? Years ago these choices were unrealistic for women; now my daughter can wish upon a star—and then become one. The freedom of choice is great."

Getting to this place of opportunity has not been easy. Hard-fought battles waged by strong-willed women over long periods of time have allowed modern daughters to improve their lot. A girl in America today can have a room of her own, a voice of her own, and an individual identity in a world once governed by stereotypes, glass ceilings, and imposed restrictions. The blood, sweat, and tears of women who courageously stared down repression have given rise to a new day. No longer is every woman's place in the home. "We've come a long way, baby" is literally true for every girl.

In this climate, every daughter owes a debt to the women before her who made sacrifices. Maybe the nineteenth-century French writer Colette expressed it best when she wrote, "Whenever I feel myself inferior to everything about me, threatened by my own mediocrity, frightened by the discovery that a muscle is losing its strength, a desire its power, or a pin the keen edge of its bite, I can still hold up my head and say to myself, 'Let me not forget that I am the daughter of a woman who bent her head, trembling between the blades of a cactus, her wrinkled face full of ecstasy, over the promise of a flower, a woman who herself never ceased to flower, untiringly, during three quarters of a century.'"

Had Colette's mother lived to witness her child's success, surely she would have agreed that a daughter is a gift.

The Gift of Mother's Helper

"They talked like girls do,

fond and late."

—EMILY DICKINSON

ith thirty guests about to descend for holiday dinner, Mrs. Benson was sprinting toward the finish line with minutes to spare and much to do, when she felt the rhythmic tug of a little hand on her red-checkered apron. "Please, mama," came the soft but insistent voice of five-year-old Jeanette. "Do you have a job for me to do? I want to help."

"Get a stool, little one," Mrs. Benson echoed back, aware that such "help" would create inevitable delays. But as she looked into the little girl's eyes, full of expectation and wonder, she remembered the words spoken years earlier by Great Grandmother Eloise,

who said that, "In a kitchen of love, every heart and helping hand is welcomed."

It is a truism of parenting. And nearly every mother knows it. Young girls like to help out, especially in the kitchen, and especially at holiday time when the place is bubbling over with fevered activity. Drawn to the frantic energy of electric mixers and Cuisinarts; the mystery of cracking eggs and measuring liquids; and the mechanical magic of rolling pins and weighing scales, "mother's little helper" is ready to befriend every biscuit batter, cake mix, and pudding pie.

"My girls line up for an assignment as soon as I pull out my recipe box," one mom recently confided. "Of course we enjoy eating what we make. Who could resist 'Grandma's Own' stuffing or yam pie with nuts and currants? But for mothers and daughters, cooking is about more than food. Gathering together, side by side, in a toasty kitchen full of good smells, goes beyond the 'pleasures of sugar and spice.'"

It's true. And, for centuries, mothers and daughters have known it. Kitchen magic exceeds exotic entrees, delicious desserts, and family favorites conjured up from dog-eared recipes wedged into old books. The hidden ingredient in every happy kitchen is the kinship of women with their sleeves rolled up and arms covered in flour, who are serving up intimacy, camaraderie, and affection.

"Peeling vegetables and kneading bread dough allows us time to share small talk and big secrets," one grown daughter said recently. "Momma will tell a story—sometimes a well-worn saw—and we all laugh until our sides split. Making messes and cleaning up, experimenting with new flavors and seasoning, we 'talk like girls do—fond and late,' bonding as we go."

Into this culture, every daughter arrives as an apprentice. Beginning with small jobs like mashing potatoes and rinsing vegetables, she may work her way up to her first homemade cake. Or she may choose to experiment, with mother by her side to steady the mixing bowl, advise about oven temperatures, and make sure that the meringue stiffens. Soon the little girl who once contented herself with licking the icing bowl is advocating for an exotic flambé or a three-tiered wedding cake frosted with edible pearls, pink flowers, and a rainbow archway spanning the bride and groom.

But, long before the wedding march rings out, a little girl must say the words: *Please, can I help?*

"When she asks," Mrs. Benson explains, "she is really inquiring if she can *belong*. Having a little girl underfoot in a madcap kitchen may be inconvenient, but it's an important rite of passage."

That's why, even in the heat of the holiday rush, a mother creates a role for each new recruit. Turning a willing daughter into an able helper may call for a pinch of motherly affection. But as the notorious Jean Brodie once said about young women, "Give me a girl at an impressionable age and I'll make her mine."

In the kitchen—a true laboratory of love—mothers do make an impression, all the while acknowledging that daughters are gifts sweeter than sugar cookies!

The Gift of
Seeing in the Dark

*"I will uphold my ideals, for perhaps
the time will come when I shall be able
to carry them out."*

—ANNE FRANK

*O*nce upon a time, when a woman's place was in the home and girls were expected to get married and have children as soon as the right fellow came along, nobody talked about girl power. Slogans such as "It's great being a girl!" or "Girl Power!" were not in vogue or, for that matter, even in existence. The inalienable rights of women to vote, receive equal pay for equal work, and be fairly protected under the law were not on the radar screen of a male-oriented society.

Then, slowly, a new era dawned. Ushered in by women of courage, daring, and vision, this time of profound change was born of discontent and dissatisfaction

felt by the "daughters of time" who understood that one voice raised loud and clear could initiate a new song. And soon, the chorus of other voices would join in.

Shh! The daughters of time are singing their songs. Let's listen to some of the messages they have delivered about integrity, responsibility, idealism, optimism, and hope:

Rebecca West: "People call me a feminist whenever I express sentiments that differentiate me from a doormat."

Betty Friedan: "It is easier to live through someone else than to complete yourself. The freedom to live and plan your own life is frightening if you have never faced it before. It is frightening when a woman finally realizes that there is no answer to the question 'who am I' except the voice inside herself."

Isadora Duncan: "The finest inheritance you can give to a child is to allow it to make its own way, completely on its own feet."

Adrienne Rich: "Responsibility to yourself means that you refuse to sell your talents and aspirations short, simply to avoid conflict and confrontation. And this, in turn, means resisting the forces in society which say that women should be nice, play safe, have low professional expectations, drown in love and forget about work, live through others and stay in the places assigned to us. It means that we insist on a life of meaningful work, insist that work be as meaningful as love and friendship in our lives. It means, therefore, the courage to be 'different,' not to be continuously available to others when we need time for ourselves and our work, to be able to demand of others—parents, friends, roommates, teachers, lovers, husbands, and children—that they respect our sense of purpose and our integrity as persons."

Rosa Parks: "I had no idea when I refused to give up my seat on that Montgomery bus that my small actions would help put an end to the segregation laws in the South. I only knew that I was tired of being pushed around. I was a regular person, just as good as anybody else. There had been a few times in my life when I was treated by white people like a regular person so I knew what that felt like. It was time that other white people started treating me that way."

Madonna: "I've had the same goal I've had since I was a girl: I want to rule the world."

And let's give the last word to two young girls who had the amazing grace to see idealistically when it was dark, and others could not see at all. Endowed with the gift of vision and optimism, these two remarkable

daughters never gave up faith
that there were better times
ahead for us all:

Helen Keller: "I have an unshakable
belief that mankind's highest nature is
on the whole still dormant. The
greatest should reveal excellencies of
mind and heart which their lesser fellows
possess—hidden, it is true, but there just
the same. The unborn goodness renders it possible for
most people to recognize nobility when they see it,
as the latent poet in a reader enables him to appreciate
a fine person."

Anne Frank: "I see the world being turned into a wilderness. I hear the ever-approaching thunder, which will destroy us too. I can feel the sufferings of millions and yet, if I look up to the heavens, I think that it will all come right, that this cruelty too will end, and that peace and tranquility will return again. In the meantime I will uphold my ideals, for perhaps the time will come when I shall be able to carry them out."

For well and truly, the world can say that both of these girls practiced courage and forbearance, holding a torch to the darkened path so that all could walk with greater assurance.

The Gift of
Choosing to Climb

"I want to rule the world."

—Madonna

*G*iven a choice between jumping rope and wrestling, Georgia chose wrestling. When she was asked to decide between dungarees and a party dress, the blue jeans always won out. And if she had a chance to climb a tree to the very top or sway gently on the tree swing at the bottom, Georgia latched on to the strongest branch and began making her way up.

"She's a tomboy," Mrs. Liu, her mother, declared proudly, adding, "the textbook variety."

Though the phrase has long been bandied about to describe girls who prefer "boyish" things, some would argue that a tomboy is a fading stereotype. In today's world, where modern daughters are admired for athletic

A daughter

who can make it

to top of the tallest

maple with strength and speed

is an outstanding gift!

prowess, unisex fashions, and the rugged personal choices that challenge pigeonholing, perhaps the term has out-lived its usefulness. "Whereas once this place was full of men," attests the owner of a workout center, "half of my clients today are buff, young women, confident enough to hold their own in a street fight. Being a 'gym rat' no longer applies only to men. And nobody with a brain would dare label these women as tomboys. That way of thinking is frivolous."

Thank goodness. As twenty-first-century daughters are venturing into areas in which a previous generation feared to tread, stereotyping has yielded to new free-doms. Girls today can wear makeup—but don't have to do so to impress the boss. Girls today can wear skirts to school on a winter day—or a more sensible pair of warm pants. A woman in the gym with defined "ab" muscles who can bench press her weight is not a jock or a "tomboy." She is *awesome*. She *rules*.

But since the expression "tomboy" still surfaces from time to time to describe an "inclination," what is its derivation? How did the expression come into being?

According to the "Take Our Word For It" website, "tomboy originally referred to a 'boisterous, rude boy,'

tom denoting 'aggressiveness associated with males.'"
Say the website editors:

"Tom was used from the Middle Ages as a term for 'common man,' based on the common name Thomas. Tomboy referring to a boisterous boy dates from before 1553. In 1579 we find it being applied to a 'bold or immodest woman,' and in 1592 it refers to 'a girl who behaves like a spirited boisterous boy.'"

Is it derogatory to call a girl a "tomboy"? It certainly used to be. One way to put girls down was to compare them to something perceived to be superior but unachievable—a girl as a cheap imitation of a boy. By nature, the human mind likes to sort and categorize information on a spectrum. In the archaic Middle Ages, that's how it was done. But times are changing. Today it's about potential, the internal human fuel that drives us to be our best selves, and to shoot for the moon. That said, as long as cruel judgments aren't attached to old labels, there is no harm in using them. That's why, when Mrs. Liu says that Georgia is a tomboy, she says it with a broad smile on her face. Mrs. Liu knows that in today's world, it takes all kinds. She also knows that a daughter who can make it to top of the tallest maple with strength and speed is an outstanding gift!

The Gift of
a Brave Heart

*"It is easier to live through someone else
than it is to complete oneself."*

—BETTY FRIEDAN

One winter evening, long after the clock on the mantle had chimed the midnight hour, a woman noticed a light burning in her twelve-year-old daughter's bedroom. Creeping in on tiptoe, she discovered the young girl asleep at her desk, clutching a paper that said: "To be nobody-but-myself in a world which is doing its best, night and day, to make you everybody else—means to fight the hardest battle which any human can fight, and never stop fighting."

Startled by the inscription, written by e.e. cummings, the woman lifted the child into bed and turned out the light. Later that night, lying awake in her own bed, she gave the matter thought.

"Dear God," the woman prayed, "please give me the strength to help my daughter when I can and to refrain when I cannot. And, most of all, please bless me with the wisdom to know the difference." With that she closed her eyes and fell asleep.

Life is funny. Though parents attempt to smooth the way in life for their children, the road is sometimes full of twists and turns leading to unexpected places. Especially in adolescence, when young girls stand poised on the threshold of womanhood, the struggle for personal identity and independence can involve some harrowing passages. "The freedom to lead and plan your own life is frightening if you have never faced it before," wrote Betty Friedan in her classic work *The Feminine Mystique,* adding that "it is easier to live through someone else than it is to complete oneself."

Let us all say an amen to that. Torn by opposing forces that pull in opposite directions, daughters on the cusp of womanhood so often feel pain and confusion. Should they be "good girls" who please their parents by following in their footsteps? Should they smile when people look at them and say that "the apple doesn't fall far from the tree"? Or will they honor the inner voice calling out to them to be bold and be their own person, even at the risk of alienating those who love them? The writer Joyce Carol Oates may have been speaking

...honor the inner voice calling out to them to be bold and be their own person...

to this conflict when she wrote in *Anteus* that, in life, "ideas brush by fleeting and insubstantial as moths. But I let them go. I don't want them. What I want is a voice."

Gaining a voice has been a struggle waged by daughters throughout time. For many, it begins by disavowing the messages of a society that still says, *Be a nice girl.... Don't make waves.... Do as mommy says.... Daddy wouldn't like it.... Don't act like a boy.... Call us more often.... Why didn't you call? ...Don't rock the boat.... No girls allowed.*

"We were taught very early on to color between the lines and be people pleasers," one daughter said. "But sometimes the lines box us in, limiting the imagination. And the "respected authority figures" haven't earned it. "The truly iconoclastic daughters understand the profound truth uttered by George Orwell who once noted that, "If liberty means anything at all, it means the right to tell people what they do not want to hear."

And so, falling asleep at their desks, our daughters may awaken to fight the battles that rock the world. And, if their parents' prayers are answered, they will know that this is how it should be, *must* be. For every daughter who dares to listen to the idealistic beating of her own brave heart is a precious gift, one each family must come to treasure.

The Gift of
the Dutiful One

"These are my daughters
I suppose. But when in the world did
my children vanish?"

—Phyllis McGinley

nlike her sisters who kept their distance, Jamie was known as the "dutiful one." Each day, regardless of where she was in the world, she called her parents to check up on them. Whenever she was at home, in their neighborhood, she ran their errands, cleaned up the dishes, and helped pay the bills. Sometimes, in flu season, she delivered homemade soup to help ward off sickness.

"I'm no saint," Jamie said, deflecting praise. "These are my parents who were always there for me, doing what was needed, when I was growing up. Now it's my turn."

When grown daughters leave home, what is expected? And what is fair? In today's culture, where the extended family is a thing of the past, more children are remote, like Jamie's siblings, rather than like Jamie. It has become commonplace for elderly parents to wind up in nursing homes and assisted-care facilities, alone and neglected, when their children live nearby in large, opulent houses. Visits to these shut-in people are rare and many suffer out the last years of their lives in quiet misery with flagging dignity. One has to wonder where the dutiful daughters are all hiding.

"Today's world is a hectic place," Jamie says, "where people practice a form of what someone in the *New Yorker* called 'conspicuous industriousness,' that lets them justify neglecting their parents by saying they are too busy. Or they remember all the mistakes their parents made when they were growing up and decide to even the score by disowning the very ones who gave them life. Well, the bottom line is that we each get two parents. And who is perfect? And if I wake up tomorrow and my parents are not here anymore, what difference will these arguments make?"

Jamie makes a good point. Being an example, not a critic, is a better way. Putting grievances aside and showing more kindness is the path to a more humane world, where one person helping one person improves the fate of all. If anybody doubts that this is the route to a better tomorrow, she should share a bowl of homemade soup some chilly winter's day with Jamie's parents, who will readily tell you that a dutiful daughter is a life-affirming gift.

The Gift of
Endless
Possibilities

"To an old father, nothing is more sweet than a daughter."

—EURIPIDES

*O*h! Please come closer. Don't be shy. With a little bit of time on our hands, we've decided to dip into our photo album of treasured memories and delicious snapshots. Do you want to take a journey down memory lane? We'd love your company. Feel free to pull up a chair as we reminisce about the life of our daughter.

Click! After months of high hopes and expectations, she's arrived! A black-and-white snapshot finds her snug in the arms of her tired but joyful parents, who stare straight into the camera, displaying their miraculous bundle of life for all eyes to behold. This is the day they have waited a lifetime to celebrate. But now that it has arrived, our girl sleeps through her first photo opportunity.

Click! A bit of time has passed and our precious little girl is taking a bath in the kitchen sink, held

tightly in the arms of her parents, who have a small towel handy to wipe any tears. As we turn the page of the album, she is laughing and playing amid a mound of soft toys. Now she's making quite a mess in a bowl of cereal. And—what's this?—baby's first steps caught on film! How she wobbled like a drunken sailor, gliding from one piece of furniture to another, in awe at her own accomplishment.

Click! Thank goodness someone had a camera at the first birthday celebration. With candles all aglow atop the cake, our mischievous girl has stuck her fingers in the icing. Watch mom make a wish and blow out the lights for the celebrant before tearing open the packages. A soft teddy bear. Warm mittens. And a copy of *Good Night Moon*.

Click! Where did the years go? The pages of the album turn and time marches forward. Now the number of pictures recording each event has begun to dwindle. A picture here and there of the school play, the family picnic, and our girl at the beach. A picture taken on class day at school. And then, a gap of time, as she assumes a more adult look. No more pigtails. No more braces. No more shiny barrettes.

Click! What's this? Our girl in cap and gown, smiling into the camera, waiting to take on the world. Lots of supportive friends are in a huddle by her side, shedding tears of joy and offering warm embraces. Is this the little girl who once scribbled on the living room wall with a crayon when no one was

54

looking? Is this the girl who once took a pair of scissors and cut her dolly's hair—and then her own? Who used to stand on her head outside the kitchen and notch the door frame to mark her height? How time has passed.

Look! This page remains blank, the rest of the story waiting to be told. Where do you suppose this little girl is destined to go as she ventures out into the world? Surely she will fulfill her parents' greatest dreams, the dreams they dreamed when she was just an idea in their heads. For truly they have discovered that having a daughter is more than a dream come true. Having a daughter is one of life's greatest gifts, the gift of endless possibilities.

My Daughter,
My Gift:
What I Love Most
about My Daughter

$\mathcal{E}$very daughter is special because every daughter is different. What is unique about yours? The following pages have been provided for you to jot down your special recollections about your daughter.

Personal Observations about Daughters

Resources

Use of the following books is gratefully acknowledged in the research and compilation of this book:

A Book of Love for My Son,
by H. Jackson Brown, Jr. and Hy Brett

A Book of Love for My Daughter,
by H. Jackson Brown, Jr., Paula Y. Flautt, and Kim Shea

A World of Ideas, by Chris Rohmann

Bartlett's Book of Familiar Quotations, 16th edition

Bartlett's Book of Anecdotes, Revised edition

*The Complete Book of Bible Quotations from the
New Testament*, edited by Mark L. Levine and Eugene Rachlis

*The Complete Book of Bible Quotations from the
Old Testament*, edited by Mark L. Levine and Eugene Rachlis

The Fabric of Friendship

Quotationary, by Leonard Roy Frank